OVER Easy

OVER

Creative Ideas for Pieced Quilt Backs

Lerlene Nevaril

Martingale®
& COMPANY

D0752105

Dedication

To all the quilters who asked, "Why don't you write a book about pieced quilt backs?" Thanks.

Acknowledgments

It's not possible to acknowledge all of the influences and contributors to my pieced quilt backs. I began by hand quilting small whole-cloth designs with printed backs so my uneven stitches would be hidden on the back. I've since come to rely on the expertise of machine quilters like Jan Korytkowski, Mary Roder, Wanda Jones, Brenda Shreve, Lyla Pack, Bonnie Lohry, and Boni Markve. My pieced backs got their start with a quilt I did for Eileen Taylor. She challenged me to make an interesting quilt back out of four different one-yard cuts of fabric and some scraps. My family and friends encouraged me by expecting something interesting on the back of my quilts. I thank you all for your support.

Over Easy: Creative Ideas for Pieced Quilt Backs
© 2006 by Lerlene Nevaril

That Patchwork Place® is an imprint
of Martingale & Company®.

Martingale & Company
20205 144th Avenue NE
Woodinville, WA 98072-8478 USA
www.martingale-pub.com

Printed in China
11 10 09 08 07 06   8 7 6 5 4 3 2 1

Library of Congress Cataloging-in-Publication Data
Library of Congress Control Number: 2006002326

ISBN-13: 978-1-56477-675-4
ISBN-10: 1-56477-675-1

Mission Statement

Dedicated to providing quality products
and service to inspire creativity.

Credits

President: Nancy J. Martin
CEO: Daniel J. Martin
COO: Tom Wierzbicki
Publisher: Jane Hamada
Editorial Director: Mary V. Green
Managing Editor: Tina Cook
Technical Editor: Laurie Baker
Copy Editor: Sheila Chapman Ryan
Design Director: Stan Green
Illustrator: Laurel Strand
Cover Designer: Stan Green
Text Designer: Regina Girard
Photographer: Brent Kane

Contents

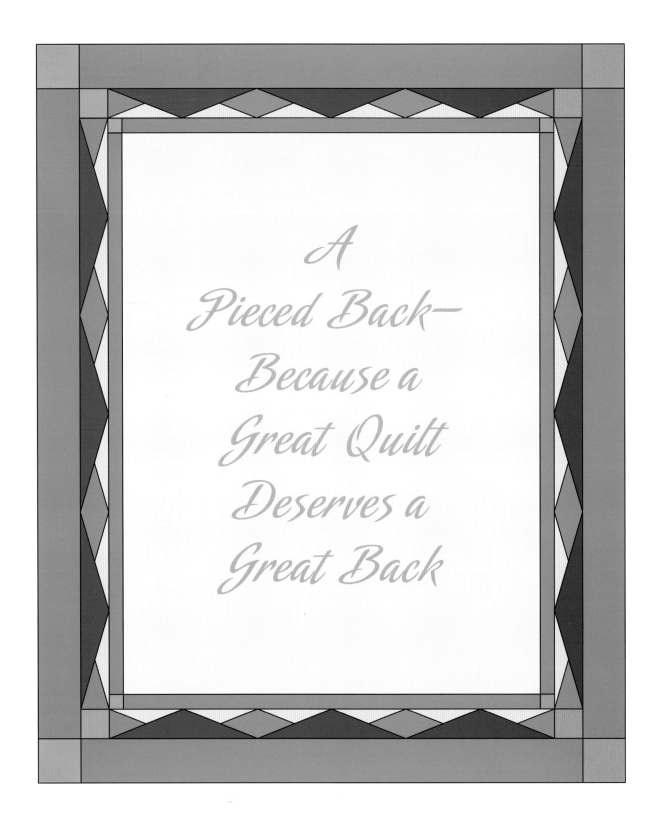

A
Pieced Back—
Because a
Great Quilt
Deserves a
Great Back

Introduction

You've worked hours on your quilt top, and it's finally finished. You've bought the batting and hired the quilter. If you're like most quilters, you're already thinking about and planning your next quilt. Stop! Take some time to consider the backing for the quilt you've just finished. What are people going to see when they turn over your beautiful top? Plain muslin? A tone-on-tone backing fabric? An unattractive fabric from the markdown table? Why not give them something unexpected, something interesting, something exciting? I'm not talking about another intricately pieced design. There are a lot of quick and easy ideas for your quilt back that you can complete in an afternoon. They range from side-by-side strips, to a single oversized block, to preprinted panels.

This book presents more than 65 photos and illustrations of actual quilt backs or ideas for quilt backs, broken down into 14 chapters. Some are accompanied by materials lists and piecing instructions. Some instructions are given in several sizes to fit a variety of quilt-back sizes. In addition, the quilt photos will set your creativity in motion.

You don't have to plan the back before you start the quilt. Often the fabrics, blocks, or units you have left over from piecing the top will spark the best idea for the quilt back. If you want the back fabrics to match the quilt top, just buy extra fabric to total the amount required for the back. Or, you could dig into your stash for coordinating fabrics.

I must warn you—once you start piecing your quilt backs, people will start expecting it and will sneak a peek at the back when you show off a new quilt! It's a fun way to try out new ideas and techniques. If your ideas don't meet your expectations, relax—you still have a great design on the front.

A Pieced Back Gives Your Quilt a Second Chance to Shine

General Instructions

The general techniques covered in this section apply to sizing and constructing any quilt back, so I recommend that you read this section before using the design ideas presented in the chapters.

Size of the Quilt Back

Using an oversized quilt back makes it easier to center the quilt top and batting on top of it, and compensates for shifts or shrinkages during quilting. Machine quilters like oversized backings because they can be easily clamped to the quilting machine.

In general, a quilt back should be 2" to 4" larger than the quilt top on each side. For example, the back for a 40" x 40" quilt top should measure 44" x 44". For a larger quilt, 70" x 70" for instance, the back should measure 78" x 78". Use these as guidelines, not hard-and-fast rules. A slight variance either way won't be a problem.

Outer Strips

Some of the quilt backs in this book are made from strips that are all the same width. To make sure that the strips on the finished project are all the same width, the outer strips should be cut 2" to 4" wider to accommodate the overall larger size of the quilt back, as explained above. Then, after quilting, the excess fabric will be trimmed away. The individual cutting instructions will specify when wider strips are required.

Yardage Requirements

Yardage requirements are not included for most quilt-back designs in the book. Hopefully you can use up bits and pieces left over from making the quilt top, or dig into your stash. That will make the backs economical as well as enjoyable to look at. If you want to use the same fabrics on the back that you used in the top, buy extra yardage of the fabrics used in the quilt top. For example, if your top uses five fabrics and the pattern tells you the back will require 2½ yards, simply buy an extra ½ yard of each of the fabrics required for the top. Or, buy greater quantities of just two or three of the top fabrics, the ones you like the best. Just make sure that the extra yardage closely matches the total yardage required for the back.

Figuring Yardage

Sometimes you want to use one long lengthwise strip for borders on the quilt top or when piecing the back. Once you cut the strip, how much yardage do you have left to be used for making the blocks? The first chart below shows you how to figure the number of square inches in your piece of fabric, subtract the square inches you use, and determine how much yardage is left. The second chart shows yardage converted to fractions and inches.

Calculating Square Inches

1 yard = 36" x 42" = 1512 square inches
Example: Cutting three strips, 6" x 36", uses 18" x 36"
18" x 36" = 648 square inches used
1512 - 648 = 864 square inches remaining
864 ÷ 1512 = .57 yard, or ½ to ⅝ yard remaining

Yardage Conversion Chart

Yard	Fraction	Inches
⅛	.125	4½"
¼	.250	9"
⅓	.333	12"
⅜	.375	13½"
½	.500	18"
⅝	.625	22½"
⅔	.667	24"
¾	.750	27"
⅞	.875	31½"
1	1.00	36"

Piecing Strips

If you are using up smaller pieces of fabric or making a bed-sized quilt back, it may be necessary to piece strips together to achieve the required length. It will save on fabric if you piece the strips using a straight, crosswise seam. Many small, overall prints, and even some large prints, can be pieced this way. Some fabric joins are more pleasing, however, when the strips are pieced with a 45°-angle seam. This is especially true when piecing two different fabric colors or designs. Be aware that piecing on the diagonal shortens the combined length by approximately the width of the strip. For example, two 8"-wide strips, each 18" long, pieced on the diagonal will yield a strip that measures only about 28", not 36". Always check before you cut and piece to make sure you will have the length you need in the pieced strip.

Using the Charts in This Book

It would be impossible to give instructions for every size of quilt back you're going to need to make. Hopefully, the sizes in this book will be close to what you need. You may need to add another strip or two, or make strips a couple of inches wider or longer. The charts will get you close; you can fine-tune the instructions to fit your individual quilt back.

In the cutting guides in the chapters that follow, a ¼" seam allowance is included in all of the measurements.

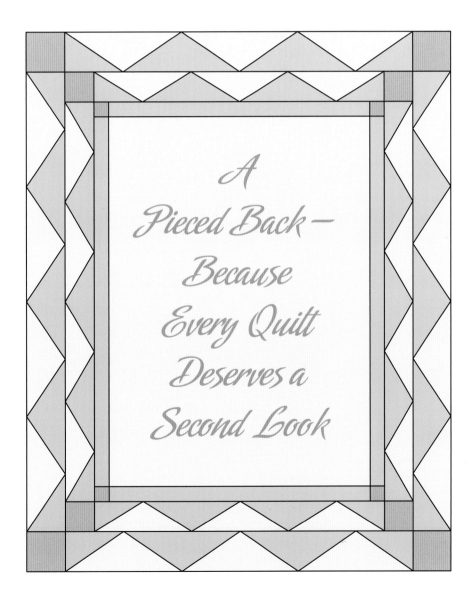

A Pieced Back— Because Every Quilt Deserves a Second Look

Expanded Blocks

When it comes to designing a great quilt back, nothing can beat the impact of making one oversized block. A 12" block from the front becomes a real scene stealer when it's blown up to 36" on the back, like the Arizona block I used on the back of the "Hydrangea Time" quilt shown here. Not only is the impact impressive, but the quilt back goes together quickly. Most large blocks can be put together in less than an hour. When was the last time you put together all of the 9" or 12" blocks for a 68" square quilt top in one hour?

It's easy to convert any block to two or three times its normal size. Simply multiply the finished size of each of the block's individual units by two or three and then add the appropriate seam allowance (½" for squares and rectangles, ⅞" for half-square triangles, 1¼" for quarter-square triangles).

Hydrangea Time *quilt back by Lerlene Nevaril, 68" x 68".*
Machine quilted by Wanda Jones.

Arizona block

Cutting Guide for the Arizona Block

Piece	12" block	24" block	36" block
Small squares	2½" x 2½"	4½" x 4½"	6½" x 6½"
Squares for half-square triangles	2⅞" x 2⅞"	4⅞" x 4⅞"	6⅞" x 6⅞"
Flying-geese units: Rectangles	2½" x 4½"	4½" x 8½"	6½" x 12½"
Squares	2½" x 2½"	4½" x 4½"	6½" x 6½"
Rectangles	2½" x 4½"	4½" x 8½"	6½" x 12½"
Center square	4½" x 4½"	8½" x 8½"	12½" x 12½"

Once you have made the enlarged block, you need to determine how much larger the quilt back needs to be and how you want to fill it in. To continue with the "Hydrangea Time" quilt back, a 4" inner border with corner squares was added to the enlarged block, and then a large final border was added. If you're short on fabric, combine two fabrics with 45°-angle seams for the final border to finish the back. Don't worry if you have to make one or two of these outer borders narrower than the others. When the quilt layers are put together, it's possible that they won't get centered exactly (and don't go crazy trying) and the borders will end up different sizes anyway.

For the "Autumn Richness" quilt back shown below, the large block is 24" x 24", twice the size of the blocks on the front of the quilt. The sizes of the first and second borders are determined by the corner squares in the large block. The corner squares repeat the design unit from the corner of the block. This is an 8" unit, so the first and second borders are each 8" wide. You can see a narrow, green third border.

Autumn Richness *quilt back by Lerlene Nevaril, 59½" x 59½".*
Machine quilted by Lyla Pack.

'30s Weathervane *quilt back*
by Lerlene Nevaril, 32" x 32".
Machine quilted by Jan Korytkowski.

The two quilt backs at right consist of large blocks, which are surrounded by strips added in the style of a Log Cabin block. (You will learn more about this style in the next chapter.) In "'30s Weathervane," the strips are all the same width. They are pieced randomly, with the second color wrapping around the corner to add to the design. The strips are cut the same width as the smallest units in the block. This keeps the border and block in proportion, and one does not overpower the other in this small wall hanging.

In "Folk Art Wheel," the strips are different widths. The random widths add interest to the design and also help to position the block off center. In this quilt back, the block is merely the pinwheel center of the Carpenter's Wheel block used on the front. You don't always have to expand the entire block.

Folk Art Wheel *quilt back*
by Lerlene Nevaril, 49" x 49".
Machine quilted by Jan Korytkowski.

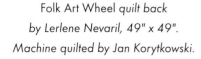

Two Color Quilt *quilt back*
by Lerlene Nevaril, 66½" x 83".
Machine quilted by Mary Roder.

Here is another quilt back where the pinwheel center of a block used on the quilt top was enlarged from 6" to 12" so that it became a large block on the back. I had bought these navy and cream fabrics at a quilt show with no specific project in mind. A pieced quilt back was the perfect place to use up the leftovers. I had enough fabric for sashing and setting squares, too. Borders were added, utilizing the background fabric from the quilt top. The navy binding adds the perfect finishing touch.

Memories from the Mills *quilt back*
by Lerlene Nevaril, 85" x 85".
Machine quilted by Jan Korytkowski.

This is a large quilt, and a good place to use long lengths of fabric. The 16" block from the quilt top was enlarged to 32" for the back. This still left a lot of space to fill. First, 8"-wide green borders were added to the block, and then 22"-wide borders were added. To make the outer borders, a length of 44"-wide fabric was cut down the middle, making this a very effective use of fabric. Once the piece was quilted and trimmed, the outer borders finished 18" wide. Watch for your favorite fabrics to go on sale. This quilt back used about 4 yards for the outer border.

Log Cabin Blocks Set Off Center

Log Cabin Blocks Set Off Center

The Log Cabin is an easy block. It can be pieced with strips of various widths. These strips can be cut from a single fabric or they can be pieced. The color placement and strip width can be varied to suit your tastes. If you have more dark fabric than light fabric, make the dark strips wide and the light strips narrow. This puts the block off center so you don't have to spend extra time centering the quilt top on the back. You can make the block larger to showcase a special piece of fabric or start off with an unused smaller block from the quilt top.

Valentine Wishes quilt back
by Lerlene Nevaril, 54" x 54".
Machine quilted
by Jan Korytkowski.

It's said that necessity is the mother of invention, and that's exactly how the "Valentine Wishes" back design, shown above, originated. I was short on light fabrics, and I wanted a design that didn't have to be centered. Log Cabin blocks are quick and easy to put together, so that's what I chose to do.

Backs with Log Cabin blocks set off center provide several benefits. As noted above, they offer the perfect use for unequal amounts of light and dark fabrics. A design that's off center is more pleasing to the eye. A centered design has more of a bull's-eye effect, and if it isn't lined up exactly in the middle, it looks all wrong.

Cutting exact logs for a Log Cabin block can take a lot of time and effort. It is easier and faster to just cut several strips and start piecing. Piecing randomly is more interesting and spontaneous. When you get to the outer edges, use wider strips. The reason for this is twofold. First, it saves time. Second, part of the last strip will get cut off anyway because the quilt back is usually 4" to 8" larger than the front.

Perfect Pansies quilt back
by Lerlene Nevaril, 48" x 48".
Machine quilted by Mary Roder.

The "Perfect Pansies" quilt back shows another Log Cabin block variation. It features a very large square set in one corner of the back so the strips are attached on only two sides. All the strips are the same size except for the outer strips. An extra-large square (24" x 24") and strips on only two sides make this 48" x 48" back superfast to piece.

Indian Puzzle quilt back
by Lerlene Nevaril, 62" x 62".
Machine quilted by Jan Korytkowski.

"Indian Puzzle" uses a block from the quilt top for the center. The color placement and strip size are random. Remember, this is a quilt back and no rules apply. The strips can be cut any size and placed in any order. You still get vibrant, interesting results.

Straight Strips

One of the easiest pieced quilt backs consists of fabric strips set side by side. The strips can be the same or different widths. They can be set together randomly or in a planned sequence. Because quilt backs are cut larger than quilt tops and then trimmed, the outer strips on the quilt back will often be a different width when the quilt is finished, and may even vary in width from one side to the other. So, feel free to do what works for you.

You should always audition the placement of strips (preferably on a design wall) to come up with the best arrangement for size and color. Make the outer strips extra wide so that they will be wide enough for quilting and final trimming. If you put 2"- to 3"-wide strips on the outer edges you may be left with only a sliver of a strip in the finished quilt; or, if the quilt back slips during quilting, the outer strip could taper down or disappear altogether.

Strip width is a matter of personal taste. Generally, wide strips look better on larger quilts and narrow strips look better on smaller quilts. However, don't be afraid to throw in an extra-wide or narrow strip for the surprise factor.

Using strips to make a quilt back is a good way to clean out your fabric stash. These backs are successful because they use a wide variety of fabrics. You can coordinate the back to the quilt top by using as few as two or three fabrics from the quilt top and pulling the rest from your stash.

For quilt backs 40" wide or narrower, all strips can be cut on the crosswise grain to save fabric. This size can be easily cut from leftover fabric from the quilt top. Strip widths from 3" to 7" look best on this size quilt back. Cut on the lengthwise grain for strips that are 42" and longer, or cut strips on the crosswise grain and piece them together. To make a rectangular back, simply increase the length of the strips, piecing as necessary.

Unless you purchase long pieces of fabric for the quilt top, or you have long pieces in your stash, strips will have to be pieced for quilt backs that are larger than 40" wide. Strip widths from 6" to 9" work best on larger quilt backs. To make a rectangular back, simply increase the length of the strips.

Straight-Strip Cutting Guide for Small Quilts

Back size	Number of strips	Strip width	Strip length
30½" x 30½"	6	5½"	30½"
39" x 39"	10	3½"	39"
	2	4¾"	39"
40" x 40"	7	4½"	40"
	2	6¼"	40"
45½" x 45½"	9	5½"	45½"
46" x 46"	12	3½"	46"
	2	5¼"	46"
48½" x 48½"	8	6½"	48½"

Straight-Strip Cutting Guide for Large Quilts

Back size	Number of strips	Strip width	Strip length
56½" x 56½"	8	7½"	56½"
63½" x 63½"	9	7½"	63½"
66" x 66"	8	6½"	66"
	2	9¼"	66"
72" x 72"	9	6½"	72"
	2	9¼"	72"
83" x 83"	9	7½"	83"
	2	10¼"	83"

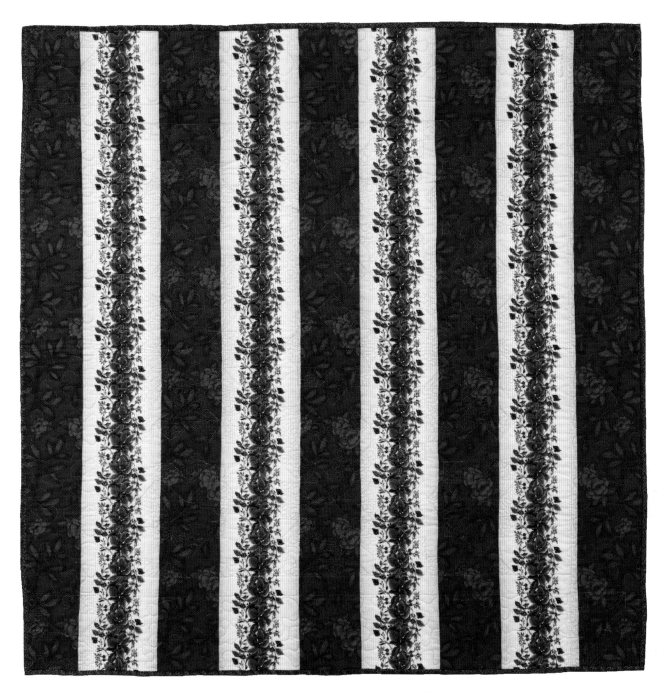

Carpenter's Wheel quilt back by Lerlene Nevaril, 49" x 49".
Machine quilted by Mary Roder.

If you use a fabric with a striped pattern, like the one in the photo, you will probably have to adjust the size of the alternate strips so that you have two different strip widths. Determine how wide your strips need to be to show the entire pattern, and then figure how wide the alternate strips need to be cut. In the quilt above, there are four striped strips that measure 6½" wide and five red strips that measure 5½" wide. Remember to cut the two outer strips wider so that the quilt back will be larger than the quilt top.

Strips of Varying Widths

If you want to use strips of various widths, try the combinations below. Cut one strip of each width and piece the strips together in the order given in the chart. To make a rectangular back, simply increase the length of the strips, piecing as necessary.

Cutting Guide for Random-Width Strips

Back size	Strip width and sequence
35" x 35"	6", 4", 5", 4½", 4", 4", 5", 6"
44" x 44"	8", 7", 4", 5", 3", 4", 7", 3", 7"
46" x 46"	7", 5", 6½", 6", 4", 5½", 4", 5", 7"
70" x 70"	12", 9", 6", 8", 7", 6", 10", 6", 10"

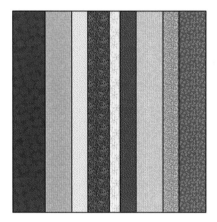

Random-width strips

Cutting Guide for Symmetrical-Width Strips

Back size	Strip width and sequence
28" x 28"	6", 3", 3", 7", 3", 3", 6"
44" x 44"	8", 5", 5", 11", 5", 5", 8"
70" x 70"	12", 8", 8", 17", 8", 8", 12"

Symmetrical-width strips

Cutting Guide for Repeating-Width Strips

Back size	Strip width and sequence
28" x 28"	6", 2½", 4", 6", 2½", 4", 6"
40" x 40"	8", 3½", 6", 8", 3½", 6", 8"
52" x 52"	10", 4½", 8", 10", 4½", 8", 10"
60" x 60"	12", 4½", 9", 12", 4½", 9", 12"
66" x 66"	13", 5", 10", 13", 5", 10", 13"

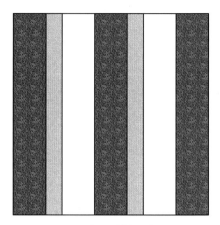

Repeating-width strips

Strips for Large Quilt Backs

On large quilt backs, using narrow strips is not very time efficient. Instead, buy one piece of fabric that's 6" to 8" longer than the quilt top and add strips to it to equal the width you need. For instance, to make an 80" x 84" quilt back, piece together 10½"-, 6½"-, 14½"-, and 10½"-wide strips to equal the length needed and then sew the strips together side by side. Sew this unit to the full-width piece of fabric.

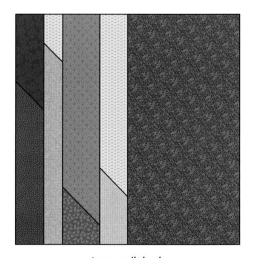

Large quilt back

Arizona Table Runner quilt back
by Lerlene Nevaril, 28" x 54".
Machine quilted by Mary Roder.

Floral Fantasy quilt back
by Lerlene Nevaril, 22½" x 47".
Machine quilted by Wanda Jones.

Here is a good design for the back of table runners. A strip-pieced back like the ones shown here makes a table runner a truly reversible item, and it takes just a few minutes more to make than it would to size and cut a single piece of fabric. The cutting measurements for the "Arizona Table Runner" are for a pieced backing that measures 4" wider and longer than the table runner top, or 32" x 58". You can use these same basic numbers for any size of back, adjusting the length and width as needed. It is best to adjust the length of the total pieced back by lengthening the end pieces, keeping the center

strip and the strips immediately above and below it the same width. You can make the end pieces the same width or different, depending on your preference.

Cutting Guide for "Arizona Table Runner" Back (To Fit a 28" x 54" Finished Quilt)

Pink strips	12½" x 32" (cut 2)
Blue strips	6½" x 32" (cut 2)
Center strip	22½" x 32"

Fancy Feathers *quilt back, made and quilted by Lerlene Nevaril, 20" x 20".*

This is another variation on the same theme. It is an easy solution to what to do with small, leftover strips. Sometimes it only takes a small effort to make a big impact. Appliquéing a few feather tips across the seam lines and in the center strips really adds pizzazz.

A
Pieced Back—
Give Your Quilt
a Second Chance
to Make a Good
First Impression

Strips at Right Angles

Strips at Right Angles

In the previous chapter, backs were shown that were made of strips running in one direction only. Fabric strips can be pieced together in sets, and these sets can be sewn together at right angles to each other. The horizontal strips can be placed to the side of the vertical strips; or a single horizontal strip, or set of strips, can be inserted into the middle of sets of vertical strips. It's your quilt—make it your way.

The chart below shows specific cutting measurements for four quilt sizes. Piece the horizontal strips together top to bottom in the order shown, and then add the vertical strips to one or both sides of the horizontal unit.

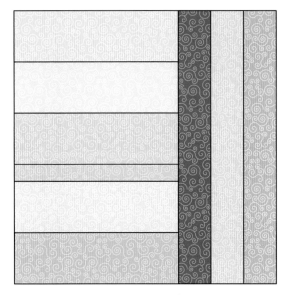

Strips on one side

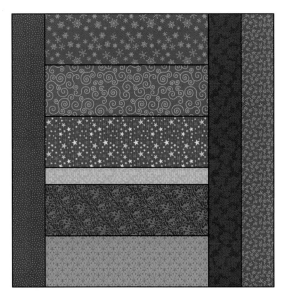

Strips on both sides

Cutting Guide for Right-Angle Strips on the Side(s)

Back size	Horizontal strips	Vertical strips
32" x 32"	6" x 20"	4" x 32"
	6" x 20"	4" x 32"
	6" x 20"	5½" x 32"
	4½" x 20"	
	6" x 20"	
	6" x 20"	
48" x 48"	9" x 30"	6" x 48"
	9" x 30"	6" x 48"
	9" x 30"	7½" x 48"
	5½" x 30"	
	9" x 30"	
	9" x 30"	
64" x 64"	12" x 40"	8" x 64"
	12" x 40"	8" x 64"
	12" x 40"	9½" x 64"
	6½" x 40"	
	12" x 40"	
	12" x 40"	
80" x 80"	15" x 50"	10" x 80"
	15" x 50"	10" x 80"
	15" x 50"	11½" x 80"
	7½" x 50"	
	15" x 50"	
	15" x 50"	

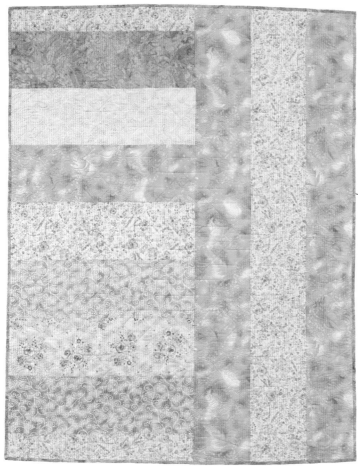

Lavender Sachet *quilt back*
by Lerlene Nevaril, 51" x 64".
Machine quilted by Wanda Jones.

This quilt was made following the cutting guides on page 20. To make the back rectangular, however, I simply added more horizontal strips and extended the length of the vertical strips.

Diamond Stars—Wild and Crazy *quilt back*
by Lerlene Nevaril, 42" x 42".
Machine quilted by Bonnie Lohry.

Horizontal and vertical strips were both used for the "Diamond Stars—Wild and Crazy" backing, but the arrangement is slightly different than shown in the cutting chart. Because I used a lot of scraps, the vertical strips weren't quite long enough by themselves. That was easily corrected by joining pieces for one strip and adding a horizontal strip to the end of the others. This is a great way to whittle down your stash.

To take advantage of shorter fabric lengths, you can put a horizontal strip in the middle. The cutting guides at right show different strip widths for the top and the bottom halves. If you want, you can use just one set of strip widths for both the top and bottom. If you choose this option, you must still cut the strips at the given vertical lengths to have enough length. To make a rectangular quilt back, simply add to the vertical strip lengths. The horizontal strip looks best if it is placed off center, so keep this in mind when adding length to the strips.

One strip in the middle

Cutting Guide for One Horizontal Strip

Back size	Vertical strips (top half)	Horizontal strip	Vertical strips (bottom half)
48" x 48"	6" x 15"	10" x 48"	9" x 24"
	3" x 15"		3" x 24"
	6" x 15"		12½" x 24"
	12½" x 15"		6" x 24"
	6" x 15"		6" x 24"
	6" x 15"		6" x 24"
	6" x 15"		3" x 24"
	6" x 15"		6" x 24"
64" x 64"	8" x 20"	13" x 64"	12" x 32"
	4" x 20"		4" x 32"
	8" x 20"		15½" x 32"
	15½" x 20"		8" x 32"
	8" x 20"		8" x 32"
	8" x 20"		8" x 32"
	8" x 20"		4" x 32"
	8" x 20"		8" x 32"
80" x 80"	10" x 25"	16" x 80"	15" x 40"
	5" x 25"		5" x 40"
	10" x 25"		18½" x 40"
	18½" x 25"		10" x 40"
	10" x 25"		10" x 40"
	10" x 25"		5" x 40"
	10" x 25"		10" x 40"
	10" x 25"		10" x 40"
96" x 96"	12" x 30"	19" x 96"	18" x 48"
	6" x 30"		6" x 48"
	12" x 30"		21½" x 48"
	21½" x 30"		12" x 48"
	12" x 30"		12" x 48"
	12" x 30"		6" x 48"
	12" x 30"		12" x 48"
	12" x 30"		12" x 48"

The final variation simply splits the horizontal strip into two strips. Use the previous vertical-strip guides and plug in the new horizontal-strip cutting sizes below. The total width of the horizontal strips is still the same. To convert a square back to a rectangular one, add more horizontal strips or add to the length of the vertical strips.

Cutting Guide for Two Horizontal Strips

Back size	Top horizontal strip	Bottom horizontal strip
48" x 48"	6" x 48"	4½" x 48"
64" x 64"	8" x 64"	5½" x 64"
80" x 80"	10" x 80"	6½" x 80"
96" x 96"	12" x 96"	7½" x 96"

Two strips in the middle

Ripples in the Stream quilt back by Lerlene Nevaril, 75" x 75". Machine quilted by Mary Roder.

I had originally pieced together vertical strips for the "Ripples in the Stream" quilt back, but the result didn't have much graphic appeal. By cutting the back horizontally and adding the green strip, the quilt back suddenly packed a punch. Sometimes you just need to inject a spot of high contrast to make your quilt back shine.

Brown and Blue Geese *quilt back by Lerlene Nevaril, 73" x 73".*
Machine quilted by Wanda Jones.

"Strips for Large Quilt Backs" on page 16 illustrates a large quilt back made using a full-width length of fabric with narrow strips on one side. For the "Brown and Blue Geese" back shown above, the large piece of fabric is in the middle and short strips are sewn together and placed on both sides. This is a great way to use up some of those fat quarters you bought and never used because they weren't big enough.

A
Pieced Back—
It's Not Just a Back
It's Another Quilt

Chinese Coins

Chinese Coins, Roman Stripe, or Bars—call this design whatever you want. In one form or another, this strip-quilt design has been around since 1850. It makes a perfect candidate for a quilt back. It can be made any size, determined by the size of your fabric pieces, the size back you need, or the leftover blocks you want to include. Chinese Coins backs consist of wide pieced strips set between narrow strips of a single fabric. The rectangles, or "coins," that make up the pieced strips are various-length segments sewn into a vertical strip.

The "Indonesian Splendor" quilt back on the facing page began with a leftover block from the top. The block was 9", and that became the width of the coin strips. Cutting the pieces for the strips in different lengths made the most efficient use of the fat quarters left over from piecing the top. The number of columns and the width of the spacer strips were determined by the size of the back. There is no hard-and-fast rule to follow. The outer spacer strips were cut wider to make the back large enough. The length of the coins ranges from 1½" to 6½". Vary the sizes and colors of the coins so that no particular pattern evolves. This is supposed to be a one-day project, not another long-term effort.

Below are material lists and yardage guidelines for five backing sizes.

Cutting Guide for Chinese Coins Backing

Back size	Coin strips	Total coin yardage	Spacer strips	Total spacer yardage
48" x 48"	4 strips, 48" long. Cut coins 8½" wide x 2" to 5½" long.	1⅝ yards	4 strips, 2½" x 48" 2 strips, 4¼" x 48"	⅞ yard
67" x 67"	5 strips, 67" long. Cut coins 9½" wide x 2" to 6½" long.	3¼ yards	4 strips, 3½" x 67" 2 strips, 5¼" x 67"	1½ yards
51" x 70"	5 strips, 70" long. Cut coins 7½" wide x 2" to 5½" long.	2½ yards	4 strips, 2½" x 70" 2 strips, 4¼" x 70"	1¼ yards
80" x 80"	6 strips, 80" long. Cut coins 9½" wide x 2½" to 8½" long.	4½ yards	5 strips, 3½" x 80" 2 strips, 5¾" x 80"	1⅞ yards
90" x 108"	7 strips, 108" long. Cut coins 10½" wide x 2½" to 8½" long.	7½ yards	6 strips, 2½" x 108" 2 strips, 4¼" x 108"	2¼ yards

Indonesian Splendor *quilt back by Lerlene Nevaril, 68" x 68".*
Machine quilted by Wanda Jones.

Simple Squares

What could be easier than piecing together plain squares to make a quilt back? Throw in a few leftover blocks for interest and the results are even better. No rules apply when using squares, but it is more effective if large squares are arranged in a definite color sequence. For a charming effect, randomly arrange small squares to make your quilt back.

The "Holiday Magic Mystery" quilt back shown below is an enlargement of a 4" corner square on the front of the quilt. The 1" squares on the quilt front were enlarged to 15" on the back. Sometimes even the simplest idea can make an interesting design for a back.

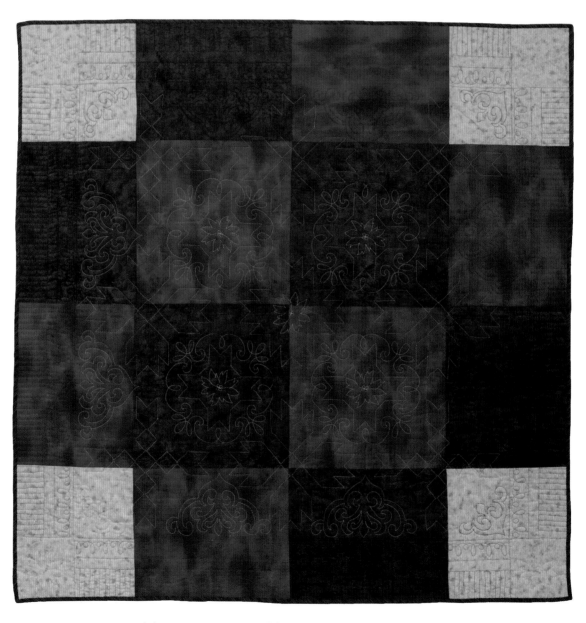

Holiday Magic Mystery *quilt back by Lerlene Nevaril, 55" x 55".*
Machine quilted by Mary Roder.

Dark Treasures quilt back by Lerlene Nevaril, 57" x 75".
Machine quilted by Wanda Jones.

The "Dark Treasures" quilt back began with four 9" blocks that weren't used in the quilt top. You will notice there are several split-square blocks on the back. Splitting some of the plain squares makes use of smaller pieces of fabric and also adds design interest to the back.

The squares in these two backs illustrate that square size and back size do not have to be proportional. Large squares were used for "Holiday Magic Mystery," which is a smaller quilt. This shows that guidelines are not strict rules. The guidelines here are meant as a catalyst to help you start planning your own quilt backs.

Surround the Units

An experienced quilter will tell you it's a good idea to make a sample of each different block in a quilt to make sure the instructions are correct—you want to locate possible errors *before* you cut all your fabric. Another good reason to make sample blocks is to make sure you like your fabric choices.

Leftover, sample, and test blocks can be used in the quilt back. By sewing frames or borders around the blocks, you can quickly piece together an interesting back. Frame large fabric motifs in place of, or to coordinate with, pieced blocks. Use various-width strips to frame the pieces so you can trim odd-sized blocks to a uniform size.

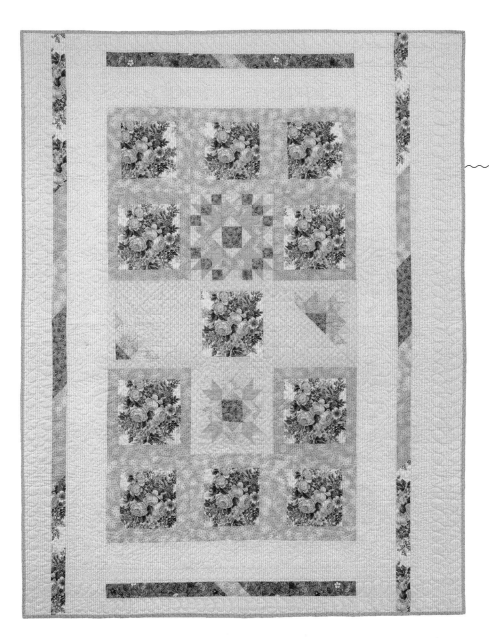

Through the Years quilt back by Lerlene Nevaril, 52" x 65". Machine quilted by Jan Korytkowski.

Samples of the pieced blocks were made for this quilt's top, and I decided not to use the block with turquoise fabric. The back, however, was another story. To pull in more of the fabrics used in these blocks, floral bouquets from one of the fabrics were framed in turquoise and pink and used as blocks. In the middle row, the leftover half-square and quarter-square triangles were used. The border area was created from colored strips that were simply inserted between wide beige strips to add color and interest. They were then added to the quilt back as a single strip. This is an easier, faster technique than making three separate borders.

Blended Beauty quilt back by Lerlene Nevaril, 51" x 64".
Machine quilted by Jan Korytkowski.

Five simple blocks form the center column of this quilt back. They are framed by a striped fabric that didn't work on the quilt top. The rest of the back is simple: plain and pieced strips. The two inner pieced strips were made by joining pieces at 45° angles. Notice how much more pleasing this angled join is than the horizontal joins on the two outer strips. The horizontal joins on the outside were necessary because that was the last of the fabric. Don't let problems like this derail the process. Improvising makes better designers and quilters.

Toile of the Day quilt back by Lerlene Nevaril, 45" x 45".
Machine quilted by Mary Roder.

Framing these test blocks gives them added importance and makes them stand out more on the quilt back. The two columns of blocks are offset, which also adds a sense of motion.

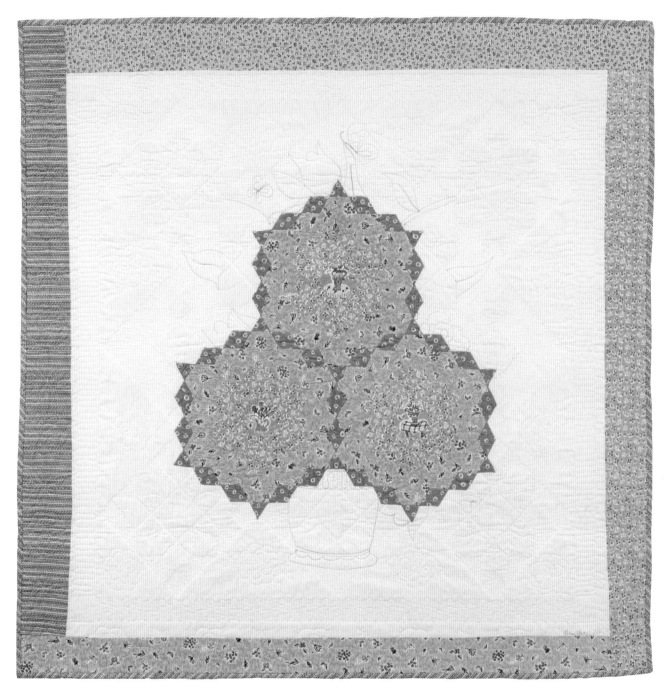

*Face in the Purple Vase quilt back by Lerlene Nevaril, 50" x 50".
Machine quilted by Mary Roder.*

The blocks you use on the back don't need to have anything to do with the quilt top. These Grandmother's Flower Garden blocks were the result of a quilt-guild class on paper-pieced hexagons. The technique was fun, and I'm glad I know how to do it, but three blocks were all I wanted to make. They were appliquéd to a square of the quilt-back fabric and then borders were added. If you only have enough fabric for three borders in one print, use a different print for the fourth border. Or, use a different print for each border.

Have you ever been in a quilt shop, fallen in love with a fabric, and bought a yard just to have it on hand? Or maybe you only bought a fat quarter…to go along with the rest of the collection that you're going to make something out of someday. You want to use these fabrics, but one-yard cuts aren't ever quite enough for a border or major design fabric, so they just sit on the shelf, gathering dust. The fat quarters are in the same boat. There they all are, just waiting for you to put them to good use. Great backings are waiting.

In this chapter, "Wonderful Yards," below, gives step-by-step instructions for making a 78" x 94" quilt back from one-yard cuts. "Fabulous Fat Quarters" on page 37 tells how to make a 40" x 48" back from fat quarters. If these backing dimensions fall just a couple of inches short in one direction or the other, don't worry. Just slash the fabric again and add another strip. Or if you're more than just a few inches short, maybe you need to add more one-yard or fat-quarter cuts.

Wonderful Yards

Here's a quick recipe for making a quilt back with left-over scraps and four of your one-yard cuts. In no time at all you will have a large back that measures 78" x 94".

1. Cut the leftover scraps from your quilt top or scraps from your stash into 2½"-wide strips. Randomly sew them together at a 45° angle to make one long strip. You will need approximately 500".

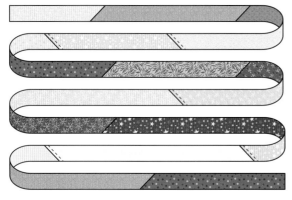

45° pieced strip

2. Arrange the four one-yard cuts as shown with the 36"-long side running horizontally.

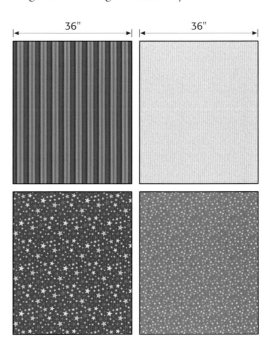

3. Cut horizontally across each one-yard piece. This is a forgiving technique. It doesn't matter where you cut, but cut in a different place on each piece.

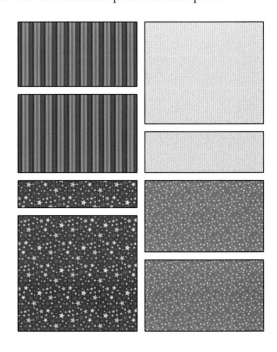

34

4. Cut six 36" lengths from the long pieced strip. Sew a strip between the cut pieces of each one-yard piece to connect them.

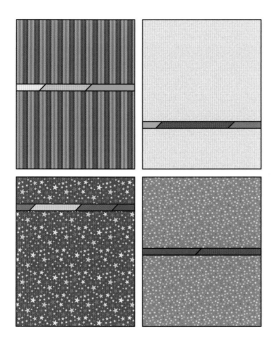

5. Now, sew another 36" length between each pair of top and bottom pieces.

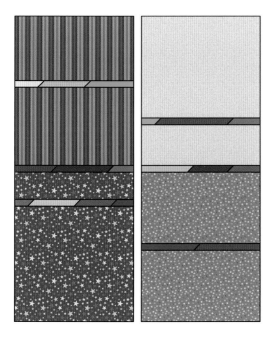

6. Measure the length of one of the halves and cut three lengths of the pieced strip to this measurement. Sew the two halves together with one length of the pieced strip between them.

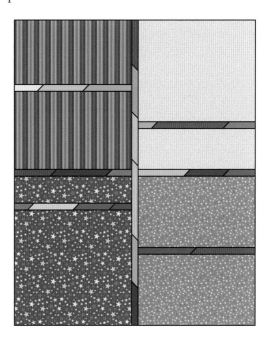

7. Make a cut the length of both panels on each side of the center pieced strip.

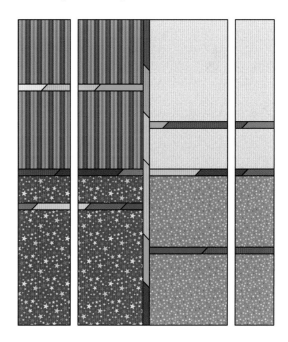

8. Sew the pieces back together, inserting a length of the pieced strip between them.

We all know that every quilt is a different size, and no one formula works for every quilt back. There are always several options. The backing for "Pastel Dreams," shown below, was modified from the previous instructions to come up with the correct size. Extra vertical strips were added and the horizontals were deleted in two quadrants. The strips were still cut 2½" wide. Make a diagram to see where and how many strips you will need in order to make the back the correct size. Remember that you are making the back 4" to 6" larger than the top. Don't place your strips so close to the edge that they will be cut off in the final quilt. The strips look more interesting if they are offset among the pieces.

Pastel Dreams quilt back by Lerlene Nevaril, 69" x 86". Machine quilted by Lyla Pack.

Fabulous Fat Quarters

What if you're making a small wall quilt? Replace the one-yard cuts with fat quarters, forming a grid with strip inserts as outlined on pages 34–36. This will give you a quilt back that measures 40" x 48".

"Patriotic Stars," below, presents another variation on piecing quilt backs from fat quarters. The quilt back is 27½" x 42". The background pieces were two fat quarters cut in half. The pieced strips were cut 2" and 3½" wide. The vertical cuts on each quadrant were made before the top and bottom pieces were put together.

Patriotic Stars *quilt back*
by Lerlene Nevaril,
24" x 36".
Machine quilted by
Brenda Shreve.

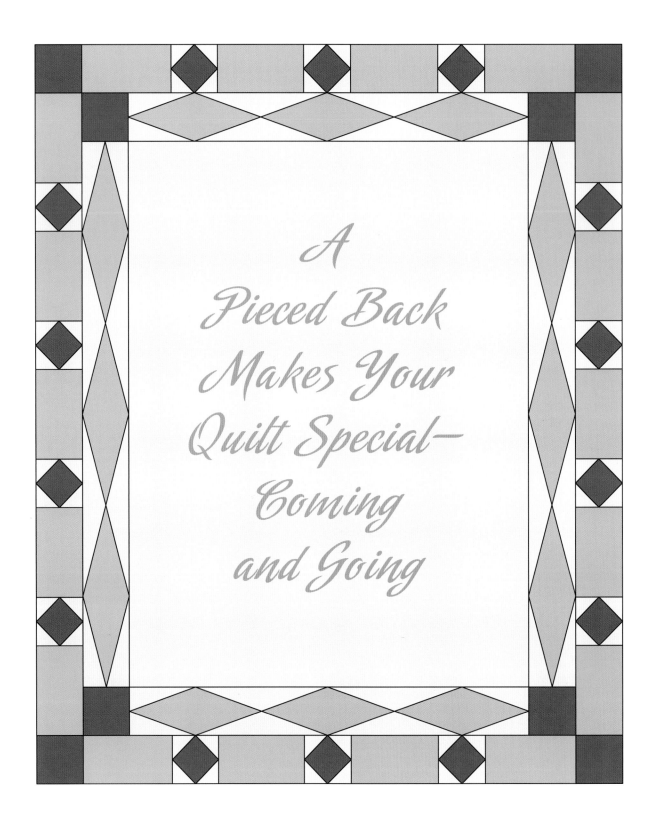

A
Pieced Back
Makes Your
Quilt Special—
Coming
and Going

Flag designs are one way to honor your heritage through quilting. Reproduce your state or national flag for the back of your quilt. Modify intricate designs for simple graphic appeal.

"Texas Liberty," shown below, is the quilt that inspired this chapter. I wanted to hand quilt a Statue of Liberty quilt top on a trip home to Texas. So why not piece the Texas flag to use for the back? Then when I began to research state flags for this chapter, I realized few state flags are good candidates for simple piecing. Many, like the Oklahoma and Iowa flags, have a pictorial design in the center. These would be major appliqué projects, much too involved for a quilt back. You want to save that kind of effort for the front of the quilt!

Texas Liberty *quilt back, made and quilted by Lerlene Nevaril, 12" x 18".*

I did work out a solution. I transferred 6" x 8" pictures of the flags to fabric, combining four images to piece a design in the center of a small (36" x 36") back. On the "Oklahoma" quilt back, below, the flags were set two by two, separated by sashing. The stripes in the "Iowa" flag, on the facing page, were perfect for a partial seam unit. This gives a little more sparkle to the design for very little extra effort. The Web site www.netstate.com is a great resource for state flags.

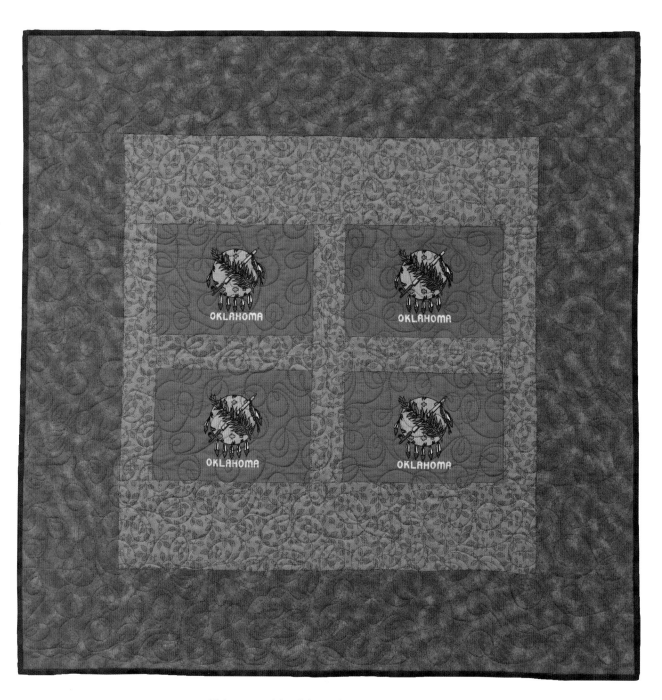

Oklahoma quilt back by Lerlene Nevaril, 36" x 36".
Machine quilted by Brenda Shreve.

*Iowa quilt back
by Lerlene Nevaril,
36" x 36".
Machine quilted
by Brenda Shreve.*

Alaska's state flag can be reproduced by machine appliquéing gold stars to a blue background.

For Colorado's state flag, join white and blue fabrics and machine appliqué a gold circle and a red *C* in the center.

Flag designs do not have to be literal. To make Mississippi's state flag, you could use a star-print fabric instead of applying stars individually.

Alaska state flag

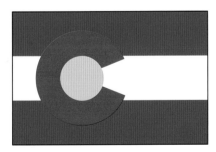

Colorado state flag

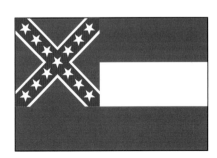

Mississippi state flag

Eagles and Stars quilt back by Lerlene Nevaril, 59" x 59".
Machine quilted by Jan Korytkowski.

The American flag is a great candidate for an easy patriotic quilt back, such as the "Eagles and Stars" back shown above. A printed fabric was used for the blue field, and 7 stripes rather than 13 made this back go together quickly. To maintain the integrity of the flag, blue star-print borders were added. The cutting instructions are given at right.

Cutting Guide for "Eagles and Stars" Quilt Back

Blue field fabric	1 rectangle, 21½" x 24½"
Red fabric	2 strips, 7½" x 25½"
	2 strips, 7½" x 49½"
White fabric	1 strip, 7½" x 25½"
	2 strips, 7½" x 49½"
Border fabric	2 strips, 5½" x 49½"
	2 strips, 5½" x 59½"

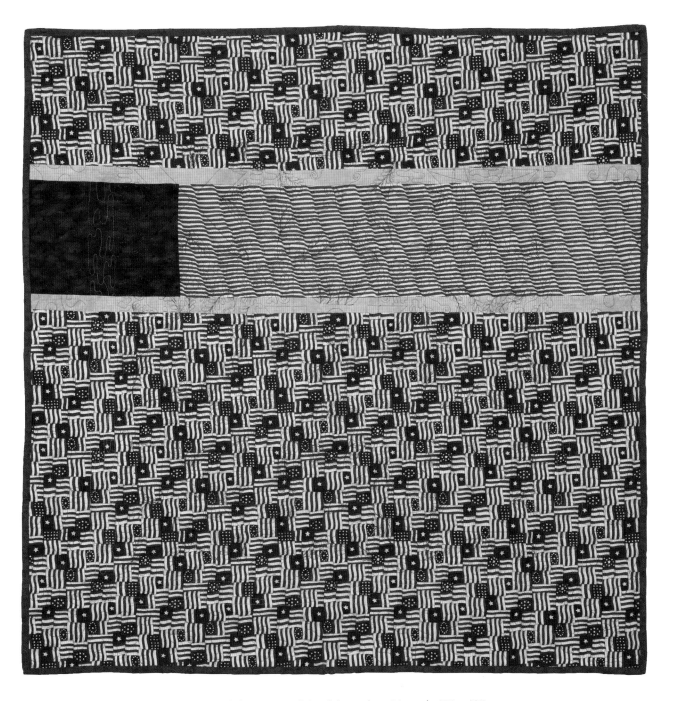

July Celebrations quilt back by Lerlene Nevaril, 42" x 42".
Machine quilted by Bonnie Lohry.

Let patriotic fabrics supply the impression of a flag, as done in the "July Celebrations" quilt back. If you trace your ancestry to another country, use that flag. Start with these ideas and see where they lead you.

Scraps of This and That

Have you ever pieced a quilt and ended up with leftover pieces and units—squares, triangles, flying-geese units, half-square-triangle units? Your conservative side tells you to save them to use later. Your practical side says pitch them—what are the chances you'll ever use them? Listen to your conservative side because you can make them into a spectacular quilt back.

All sorts of remnants and leftover units can be combined to make eye-catching quilt backs. Sew the pieces together randomly or in a planned design strip. The strip can be inserted into single-fabric quilt backs. Or, make two or three strips and randomly insert them across the quilt back. With scraps of this and that, anything goes. No piece is too small to be used. The more random the combination of units and fabrics, the more pleasing the back will be. Suddenly you have a back that gets a second look and a lot of compliments.

*Stacked Fabric Magic quilt back
by Lerlene Nevaril, 52" x 72".
Machine quilted by Boni Markve.*

When you cut out the pieces for a quilt by layering the fabric so that like motifs are stacked on top of each other, and then cut them all at once, you end up with pieces of fabric that look like Swiss cheese. Cut triangles from the leftover fabric chunks and piece them together in random order. In this example, I just started cutting and piecing triangles. I managed to use up that Swiss cheese fabric. I even had to go to my stash for the last two pieces! It felt really good to use up all the fabric.

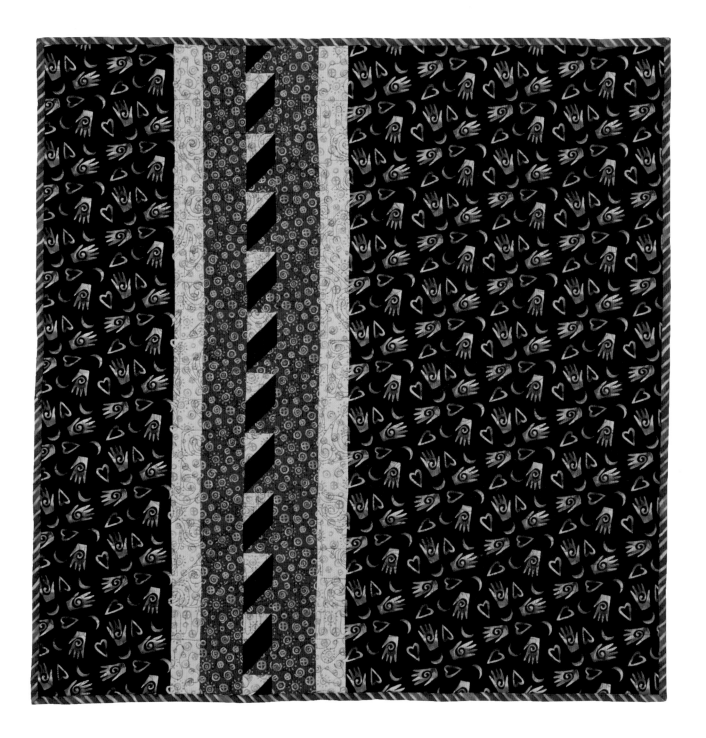

Heart and Hand *quilt back by Lerlene Nevaril, 42" x 42".*
Machine quilted by Bonnie Lohry.

Leftover half-square-triangle units can be lined up and bordered by solid strips. Set this unit off center for the most interesting look.

Candy Vanes *quilt back*
by Lerlene Nevaril, 47" x 47".
Machine quilted by Mary Roder.

The units on the front of this quilt were made from strip sets. Rather than toss the leftover strips and other fabrics from the top, I combined them for an interesting back. Alternate plain white strips and pieced strips until the back is big enough.

Flower Crowns *quilt back*
by Lerlene Nevaril, 38" x 38".
Machine quilted by Wanda Jones.

The "Flower Crowns" quilt back is very similar to "Candy Vanes." This was a guild challenge and the patterned pieces are the challenge-fabric remnants. The red/black/red units are left over from the sashing. This back, made of bits and pieces, is a graphic success.

Seventh Inning Success quilt back *by Lerlene Nevaril, 35" x 38".*
Machine quilted by Bonnie Lohry.

In the quilt above, scraps from the front are pieced
into a strip for the back. Changing the direction of the
angles adds extra interest to the strip.

The Power of Panels

The Power of Panels

Many fabric designers are now designing 22" x 44" panels to go with their fabric lines. These panels can be used to make almost instant backs. They can even be used for larger backs by using multiple panels and borders. Designs for smaller quilts consist of nothing more than a panel plus four strips added to the sides for a border. Can anything be easier?

Following are instructions for making one-, two-, and three-panel backings.

One-Panel Quilt Back

You will need one 22" x 44" panel and 3 yards of fabric for the border to make a 51½" x 66½" quilt back.

1. Trim the panel to 21½" x 42½".
2. From the border fabric, cut the following pieces:
   • 2 strips, 15½" x 42½", along the lengthwise grain, for the side borders
   • 3 strips, 12½" x 54", along the lengthwise grain, for the top and bottom borders
3. Sew the side borders to the panel first, and then add the top and bottom borders.

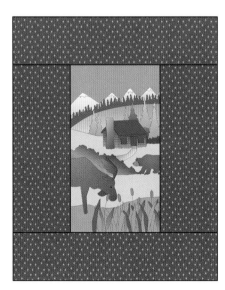

One-panel quilt back

Two-Panel Quilt Back

You will need two 22" x 44" panels, 2¼ yards of the main fabric for the border, and ¾ yard of the accent fabric for the border to make a 60½" x 76½" quilt back.

1. Trim each of the panels to 21½" x 40½".
2. From the main border fabric, cut the following pieces:
   • 6 strips, 6½" x width of fabric
   • 3 strips, 6½" x 40½"
   • 4 squares, 6½" x 6½"
3. From the border accent fabric, cut 3 strips, 6½" x width of fabric.
4. To make the center section, sew the three main fabric 6½" x 40½" strips and the two panels together, alternating the pieces as shown.
5. To make the top and bottom sections, sew the accent fabric strips together end to end to make one continuous strip. From the strip, cut 2 strips, 6½" x 48½". Sew a main fabric square to each end of the strips.
6. Sew the 6½" x width of fabric strips together end to end to make one continuous strip. From the strip, cut four strips, 6½" x 60½". Sew one strip to each long edge of the accent strips from step 5.
7. Sew the top and bottom sections to the top and bottom edges of the center section as shown.

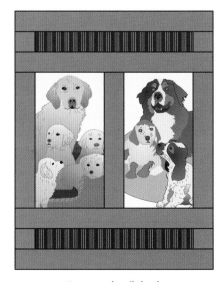

Two-panel quilt back

Three-Panel Quilt Back

To make a 100" x 100" quilt back, you will need three 22" x 44" panels, 5½ yards of fabric for the border, and 10 squares, 12½" x 12½", of assorted fabrics or simple pieced blocks that coordinate with the quilt top for the border accent.

1. Trim each of the panels to 22" x 40½".
2. From the border fabric, cut the following pieces:
   - 6 strips, 12¼" x width of fabric
   - 2 strips, 12½" x 40½"
   - 6 strips, 6½" x width of fabric
   - 2 strips, 6" x 40½"
   - 4 rectangles, 12¼" x 12½"
   - 8 rectangles, 4½" x 12½"
3. To make the center section, sew the 6" x 40½" border strips and the panels together as shown. Sew the 12½" x 40½" strips to the sides of this unit to make the center panel.

4. Sew the 6½" x width of fabric strips together end to end to make one continuous strip. From the strip, cut two strips, 6½" x 100". Sew the strips to the top and bottom edges of the center panel.
5. Sew five assorted 12½" x 12½" squares and four 4½" x 12½" rectangles together, alternating the pieces as shown. Sew 12¼" x 12½" rectangles to the ends of the strip. Make two. Sew these strips to the top and bottom edges of the quilt-back piece. If your prints are directional, be sure they are oriented in the correct direction.
6. Join the 12¼" x width of fabric strips together end to end to make one continuous strip. From the strip, cut two strips, 12¼" x 100". Add the strips to the top and bottom edges of the quilt-back piece.

Three-panel quilt back

Bright Lights quilt back by Lerlene Nevaril, 32" x 45".
Machine quilted by Wanda Jones.

Printed panels are great for smaller quilts where you only need to add one 4" to 6" border. To add interest and to use up smaller scraps, piece together random-length strips to make the border.

I fell in love with this panel immediately. I knew it would work with a red, black, and beige combination of fabrics to make a striking back. The center section, above and below the panel, was pieced with various-width strips to showcase the fabrics from the quilt top. Framing the panel with black strips helped to give it definition and finish.

"Bears in the Cabin" is a large quilt, so three panels were needed to fit across the back. Ten blocks above and below the panels are more interesting than a series of plain borders would be. That may sound like a lot to piece for a quick back, but these blocks are so simple they took less than an hour. This would also be a good place to showcase isolated images from a large print. Photo-transfer images would be another good substitute for the blocks.

Too Beautiful to Cut

All quilters do it. You go into the quilt shop and there it is—the most beautiful fabric you've ever seen. Sometimes it's the color that's so attractive, or maybe the design, or both. The bottom line is you have to have the fabric. Whenever professional quilters are asked how much fabric they buy, they usually suggest two to three yards, depending on how much you like it. So you end up buying at least three yards or more. You bring it home and go through your stash to find something to combine with it. Nothing really works, and anyway, you want to save it for a special project. Time goes by and you forget about the fabric. One day you are digging through your stash looking for a back for your latest quilt top. And there is the beautiful piece of fabric. It's the right color and almost the right size, but not quite. You could cut it up and add something else to it to make it big enough. But it's so gorgeous as a whole that you don't want to cut into it. The fabric has become a "beautiful but." It's beautiful, but you can't bring yourself to cut into it.

Here's an idea. Don't cut it into small pieces. Just add some framing strips, like you would with a painting. Even if your wonderful piece of fabric is large enough for the back, use a frame anyway. The frame lends an importance to the fabric. It tells you that there is something worth a second look inside the frame.

The center section is determined largely by the width of the fabric. Most fabrics provide 40" to 44" of usable fabric between the selvages. The frame fabric should contrast with the center fabric. The border can either repeat the center fabric or again form a contrast. Cut out the border pieces according to the diagram at right so that the pattern is going in the same direction. The layout does not provide for matching the pattern between the center panel and border, if you choose to use the same fabric. Add ¼ to ½ yard more fabric for smaller pattern repeats. Larger pattern repeats will require more fabric. Even if you aren't trying to match the pattern, all of the pieces of your "beautiful but" fabric should be cut with the pattern going in the same direction.

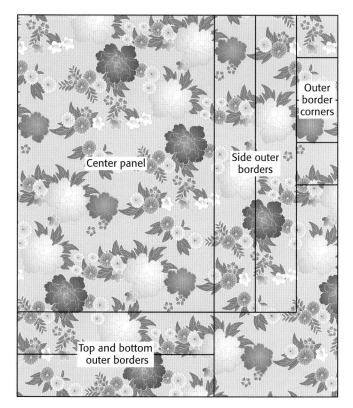

Cutting layout

Materials and cutting guidelines for three quilt sizes are given on the facing page. General instructions for making any of the backs follow the chart. To make a back slightly smaller or larger than the sizes presented here, adjust the border accordingly.

Cutting Guide for Too Beautiful to Cut Quilt Backs

Back size	Piece	Yardage	Cutting instructions
32½" x 42½"	Center panel	1 yard	1 rectangle, 21½" x 31½"
	Frame	½ yard	Vertical frame: 2 strips, 2" x 31½" 4 rectangles, 2" x 4½"
			Horizontal frame: 2 strips, 2" x 32½"
	Outer border	1 yard	Sides: 2 strips, 4½" x 31½"
			Top and bottom: 2 strips, 4½" x 21½"
			Corners: 4 squares, 4½" x 4½"
76½" x 94½"	Center panel	2¼ yards	1 rectangle, 40½" x 72½"
	Frame	1 yard	Vertical frame: 4 strips, 3½" x width of fabric; piece together and cut 2 strips, 3½" x 72½" 4 rectangles, 3½" x 8½"
			Horizontal frame: 4 strips, 3½" x width of fabric; piece together and cut 2 strips, 3½" x 76½"
	Outer border	2¾ yards	Sides: 2 strips, 15½" x 72½"
			Top and bottom: 2 strips, 8½" x 40½"
			Corners: 4 rectangles, 8½" x 15½"
90½" x 108½"	Center panel	2¼ yards	40½" x 72½"
	Frame	1½ yards	Vertical frame: 4 strips, 4½" x width of fabric; piece together and cut 2 strips, 4½" x 72½" 4 rectangles, 4½" x 14½"
			Horizontal frame: 5 strips, 4½" x width of fabric; piece together and cut 2 strips, 4½" x 90½"
	Outer border*	4¾ yards	Sides: 2 strips, 21½" x 72½"
			Top and bottom: 2 strips, 14½" x 40½"
			Corners: 4 rectangles, 14½" x 21½"

Use a different, nondirectional fabric for the outer border rather than using the same fabric you did for the center panel. Maintaining pattern direction on the outer border will require 6¾ yards instead of 4¾ yards if some pieces are cut crosswise.

1. Sew the long vertical frame strips to the sides of the panel. Sew the outer-border strips of the same length to the sides of the frame strips.

2. Join the horizontal frame strips to the top and bottom of the panel piece.

3. Sew vertical frame rectangles to the ends of the outer-border top and bottom strips. Sew outer-border corner squares to the ends of each strip. Add these strips to the top and bottom of the back.

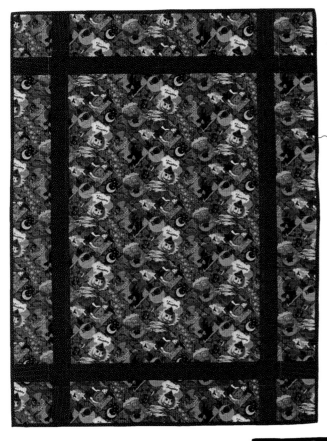

Halloween High Jinks quilt back
by Lerlene Nevaril, 34" x 44".
Machine quilted by Wanda Jones.

The frame for this small quilt was cut 2" wide. For larger quilts, cut the framing strips up to 3½" wide, as shown in "Batik Swimmers," below, and "Japanese Interlude" on the facing page.

Batik Swimmers quilt back
by Lerlene Nevaril, 48" x 56".
Machine quilted by Brenda Shreve.

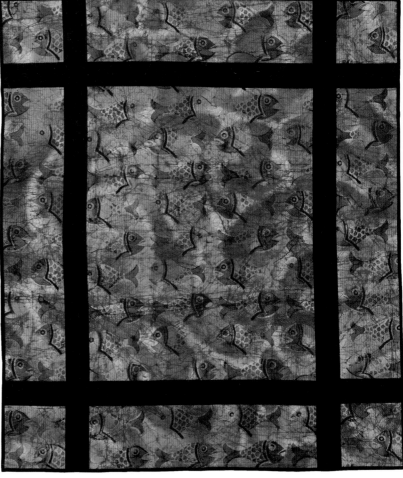

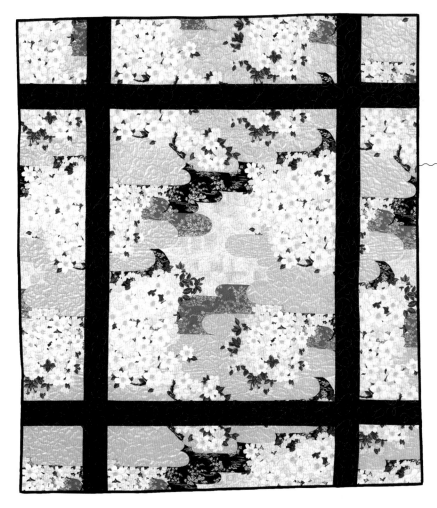

Japanese Interlude quilt back
by Lerlene Nevaril, 48" x 56".
Machine quilted by Brenda Shreve.

Garden Medley quilt back
by Lerlene Nevaril, 45" x 45".
Machine quilted by Brenda Shreve.

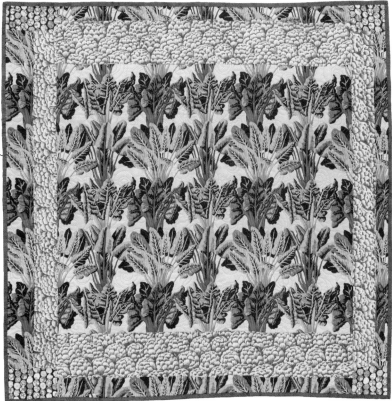

UFOs—Finally Finished

Have you taken a class or workshop and been less than wowed with the result? Take the project out of the UFO (unfinished objects) drawer and take a second look. It might be the right size and color to go with your latest quilt top. Just think how impressed everyone will be at all the piecing you did on the "back" of the quilt.

"Reproduction Rhapsody" was the result of signing up for a workshop just to be with friends for the weekend. The quilt top sat in the closet for two years. A new top made from the same fabric line brought it out of the closet again. The size was just right for the back and didn't require extra borders.

Reproduction Rhapsody quilt back; original design by Cynthie Starr.
Final design by Lerlene Nevaril, 59" x 59". Machine quilted by Mary Roder.

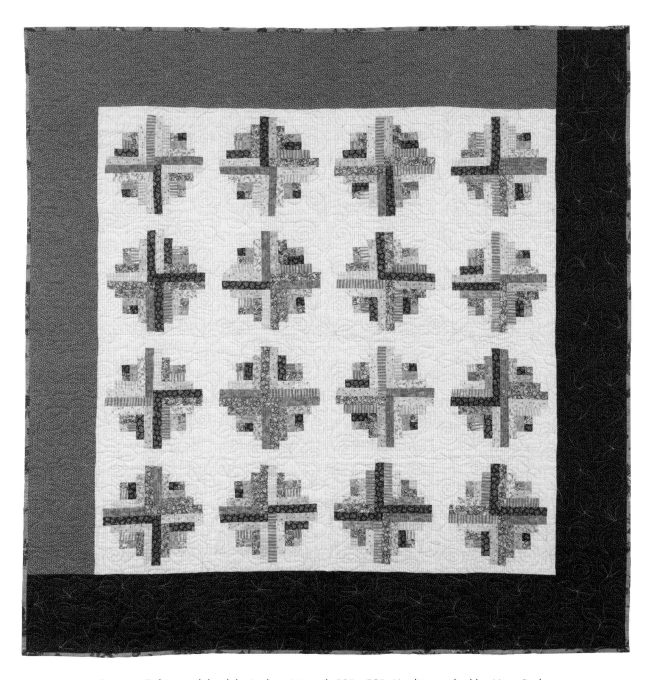

Summer Cabins quilt back by Lerlene Nevaril, 52" x 52". Machine quilted by Mary Roder.

The Log Cabin block turned me on to quilting 25 years ago, and is still a favorite. The "Summer Cabins" quilt back was originally made as a shop sample to promote a new fabric line, but it never got finished. Oversized borders from fabrics that were used in the quilt top turned this orphan into an instant, interesting back. Adding fabrics from the front that pick up some colors from the Log Cabin blocks allows two different fabric sets to work together.

If you choose a UFO for the back, choose one in which the fabrics are at least similar to those used in the quilt top, or that will coordinate with the front colors. Choose a piece for the back that is smaller than the top so you can add borders to make it larger than the top, preserving the integrity of the UFO. Using a UFO for a quilt back gives you an instant back, and one less UFO to haunt you.

Dynamite Diagonals

Dynamite Diagonals

Make a spectacular quilt back by inserting one or more strips of fabric on the diagonal. A diagonal line always adds interest to a design. A simple Nine Patch block is a static design. But substitute four half-square-triangle units for four squares, and the resulting Friendship Star block is much more dynamic.

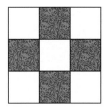
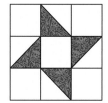

Nine Patch block   Friendship Star block

You can generate a lot more interest in a simple strip design by tossing in a diagonal or two. One word of caution: unless you cut your diagonal insert on the bias, as shown below, you will have to be aware of the stretch factor. Cutting diagonal sections on the bias ensures that the grain lines of all pieces run in the same direction, with the pieced panel's top, bottom, and side edges parallel with the less stretchy straight grain. Cutting on the bias takes more fabric than cutting on the straight grain, but it's worth it. Cutting a 5" strip to insert at a 45° angle takes 25" when cut on the diagonal and only 5" when cut straight across the fabric, selvage to selvage. Our conservative side really doesn't want to buy ¾ yard to cut a 5" strip. You can cut the 5" strip on the crosswise or straight of grain if you limit its length.

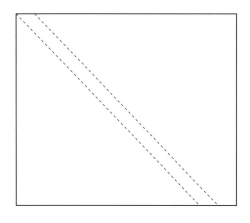

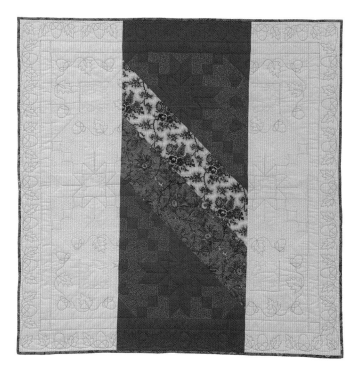

Antique Arrowheads *quilt back by Lerlene Nevaril, 44½" x 44½". Machine quilted by Mary Roder.*

Making a Quilt Back with Diagonal Strips

Following are instructions for making a quilt back that incorporates diagonal strips, as shown in "Antique Arrowheads," above. The quilt back is made up of three panels: two plain and one with diagonal strips. The side panels are cut on the lengthwise grain of the fabric. The center panel is cut on the crosswise grain. Each panel measures 18" wide.

The instructions on pages 59–60 yield a quilt back that measures 54" x 56". To change the dimensions, do the following:
- For a back wider than 54", leave the pieced panel at 18½" and cut the side panels wider. If the pieced panel were wider than 20", the inserts would have to be cut on the lengthwise grain of the fabric.
- For a narrower back, decrease the width of the side panels.
- For a longer back, increase the length of all three panels. For the center panel, add diagonal strips

and/or lengthen the top and bottom sections of the panel to reach the desired length. (If you add one more 5" diagonal strip to the center panel, this would make at least a 79"-long panel. If you want the top and bottom sections of the center panel to be longer than 40", cut 18½"-wide strips along the lengthwise grain of the fabric.)

- For a shorter back, decrease the length of all three panels. For the center panel, delete one of the diagonal strips and/or shorten the top and bottom sections to reach the desired size.

Cutting Guide for "Antique Arrowheads" Quilt Back (54" x 56")

Fabric and placement	Cutting
Fabric A (top and bottom sections of center panel)	2 strips, 18½" x width of fabric
Fabric B (top insert)	1 strip, 5½" x width of fabric
Fabric C (bottom insert)	1 strip, 6½" x width of fabric
Fabric D (side panels)	2 rectangles, 18½" x 56", cut along the lengthwise grain

1. Sew the top and bottom insert strips together along the long edges.

2. With the right side up, place one of the center panels on your ironing surface. Fold the bottom-left corner up to the right at a 45° angle as shown. Use the iron to press the fold. Fold the corner back down, and then cut along the fold line. Discard this bottom-corner piece.

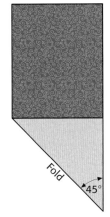

Press fold.

3. Sew the joined insert strips from step 1 to the diagonal edge of the top panel, right sides together, as shown, offsetting the pieces ¼" at point A.

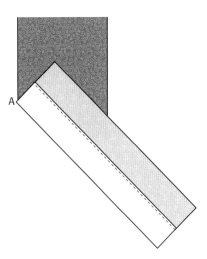

4. Press the insert down and trim the left side of the insert even with the top panel.

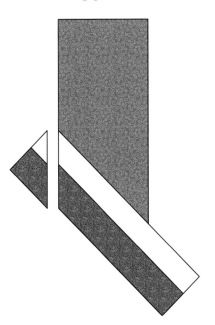

5. Place the remaining center panel on a flat surface, right side up. Fold down the upper-right corner to the left at a 45° angle; press and cut away the corner as before.

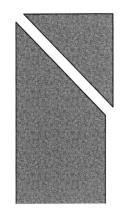

6. With right sides together, sew the bottom panel to the top panel as shown, offsetting ¼" as before on side A. Press the bottom panel down. Trim the insert even with the right side of the panel.

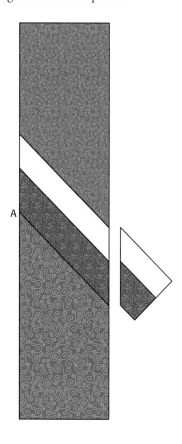

7. At this point the panel will measure about 87" long. Trim the ends so the panel measures 56" and fits the length of the side panels. Cut more off the top than the bottom so that the insert will be off center in the back. The panel looks better if the insert isn't exactly in the center. Remember, the back is cut larger than the top. Take this into account when you trim the panel so the insert does not get cut off.

8. Add the side panels to each side of the center panel.

Diagonal Design Variations

Now that you know the technique, branch out in all directions. The design below simply adds vertical strips between the panels. This is a good idea if you need to add just a little more width. These strips can be cut on the crosswise grain and pieced.

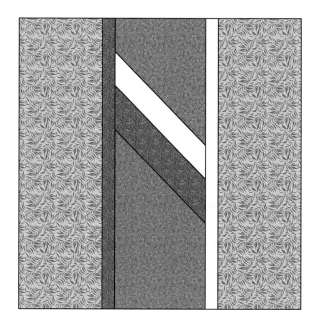

The design below uses two diagonal panels. Reversing the direction of the slant and the placement of colors adds real dimension.

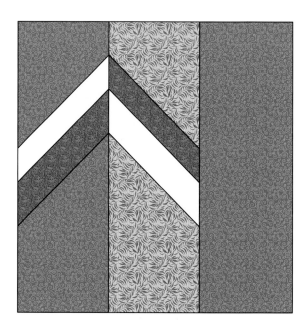

Alternating the direction of a single insert strip across three panels creates a zigzag design. The change in direction adds movement. Reversing the colors in the panels keeps the design dynamic. Another change in the design shown below is the diagonal. It is not as deep as the 45° diagonal in the previous examples.

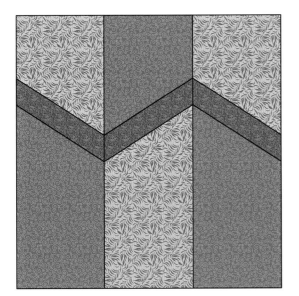

Shallow-angle panels

To make a shallow angle, simply fold up the top panel to the desired angle, press, and cut. Place the bottom panel next to it and match the fold, press, and cut. Then simply add the inserts as above. When this angle is shallower, the panels will finish to a longer length.

Cats, Cats, Cats quilt back
by Lerlene Nevaril, 44" x 62".
Machine quilted by Bonnie Lohry.

The "Cats, Cats, Cats" quilt back is different from the previous examples. This back was made up of multiple narrow strips pieced on the diagonal and enclosed by two wide panels. However, the back was not long enough. A diagonal was cut across the entire width and a pieced strip was inserted. It wasn't stable, so five strips were topstitched vertically across the insert to anchor the diagonal in place. Another great quilt back was born!

Postscript

Postscript

After studying these easy, dynamic designs, you'll never buy muslin for a quilt back again. The pieced quilt backs presented in this book are simple, eye-catching conversation starters. They use up fabric scraps, finish UFOs, and add an element of surprise. And they are just the beginning. There must be as many great backing ideas as there are quilters. Here's your chance to try something new. Step out of your box and let your imagination soar.

Enjoy!

A Pieced Back Gives Your Quilt a Back to Be Proud Of

Computer Software

Triangulations CD-ROM (software for half-square and quarter-square foundations)
Bear Paw Productions
PO Box 230589
Anchorage, AK 99523-0589
(907) 349-7873
www.bearpawproductions.com

Electric Quilt 5 (quilt-design software)
The Electric Quilt Company
419 Gould Street, Suite 2
Bowling Green, OH 43402-3047
www.electricquilt.com

Preprinted Paper-Piecing Foundations

Triangles on a Roll (half-square-triangle foundations)
HQS, Inc.
PO Box 94237
Phoenix, AZ 85070-4237
(480) 460-3697
www.trianglesonaroll.com

Custom Quilt Designs

Iowa Star Designs
Cynthie Starr
534 2nd Street
Traer, IA 50675
(319) 478-2738

Long-Arm Machine Quilters

Cottage Quilters
Wanda Jones
517 West 15th Street
Pawhuska, OK 72556
(918) 440-0488
www.cottagequilters.com

Old Dominion Quilting
Brenda Shreve
RR1, Box 1004
Barnsdall, OK 74002
(918) 847-2544

Quilting Memories and More
Jan Korytkowski
3677 N. Rawhide Circle
Castle Rock, CO 80104
(303) 663-1587

The Quiltworks
Mary Roder
518 Webster Street
Merrill, IA 51038
(712) 938-2059

Rainbow Custom Machine Quilting
Lyla Pack
841 Concord Drive
Bartlesville, OK 74006
(918) 335-2030

Valley Quilting
Bonnie Lohry
3051 Valley Drive
Sioux City, IA 51104
(712) 252-0816

About the Author

About the Author

Lerlene Nevaril discovered quilting in 1979, and in no time she was hooked. She immersed herself in the subject. She started a quilt guild and served as a regional coordinator for the Iowa Quilt Research Project.

Lerlene began teaching quilting at a local quilt shop in 1985, and has taught and lectured at shops and guilds throughout the Midwest and the South.

In 1997, with a business partner, Lerlene opened Heart and Hand Dry Goods Co., a quilt shop in Sioux City, Iowa. In 1999, Heart and Hand was one of 10 shops featured in *Quilt Sampler* magazine.

Lerlene published her first quilt book in 2002, and left the quilt shop in 2003 to free up time for more traveling and writing. This is her third book, and the ideas are still flowing.

For more information about Lerlene's teaching schedule, lectures, and classes, visit her Web site at www.lerlenenevaril.com.

A Pieced Back —
Back Your Quilt
with Beauty

01 June 2013
San Bernardino, CA
Made in the USA